JAPANESE

FOR THE BUSINESS TRAVELER

By Howard Tomb

WORKMAN PUBLISHING • NEW YORK

ACKNOWLEDGMENTS

Many thanks to Kuni Mikami and Kao Temma for their translation.

Library of Congress Cataloging-in-Publication Data
Tomb, Howard
Wicked Japanese.

1. Japanese language—Conversation and phrase books.
2. Japan—Description and travel—1945—Humor. 3. American wit and humor. I. Title.
PL539.T6   1991   495.6'83421'0207—dc20
ISBN 0-89480-862-1

Illustrations by Jared Lee
Cover and book design by Paul Hanson
Cover photo by Steve Vidler/Superstock

Workman books are available at special discounts when purchased in bulk for premiums and sales promotions as well as for fund-raising or educational use. Special editions or book excerpts can also be created to specification. For details, contact the Special Sales Director at the address below.

Workman Publishing Company, Inc.
708 Broadway
New York, NY 10003

Manufactured in the United States of America

10 9 8 7

CONTENTS

WORKING FOR THE JAPANESE

INTRODUCTION: MYSTERY AND MASTERY

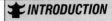

Few Westerners visit Japan for pleasure—it's farther away than Fiji, more crowded than New York, more expensive than surgery and more alien than Mars.

Many Westerners in Japan seek something more exciting and satisfying than pleasure: money. This book has therefore been geared to the traveler who wants to bring home not just meaningless snapshots and fading memories, but also fresh ink on contracts and cashiers' checks.

What follows is meant to help readers study and meditate before venturing into the arcane world of Japanese business. Careful preparation is required because many of the qualities we admire in our executives and salespeople—charm, candor, aggressiveness, unusual neckties—spell certain death in Japan.

There isn't enough room here to address the most complex questions, such as why people who are so polite urinate in the street, why they despise and admire us so deeply or how they make superior products without the help of million-dollar executives.

The purpose of this book is to help create Wicked Businesspeople who have the basic skills to get in, have some fun, carve up the opposition, and get the hell out alive.

Banzai!

INSTANT TRANSLATION GUIDE

Hundreds of English words have entered Japanese, modified to suit the Japanese tongue. There are two basic rules for proper pronunciation: consonants are always separated by a vowel, and the sounds of "r" and "l" are indistinguishable. With these rules, you can translate any English phrase into "Japlish."

Here are some classic examples.

hostess	*hosu-tesu*
beer	*beeru*
salary man	*sarariman*
nice little girl	*nigh-su ree-tu gee-aru*
hot	*hot-toh*
enormous	*ah-nolo-moo-su*
lollipop	*roh-ree poppu*
love hotel	*rabu hoteru*
Lolita complex	*rorita compa-rekusu*

THE FOUR MAJOR BELIEF SYSTEMS: BUDDHISM, SHINTO, LIFO AND FIFO

The underlying philosophies that guide our lives are alien to Japanese thinking, including the concepts of good and evil, right and wrong, and generally accepted accounting principles. As a result, the Japanese feel comfortable subscribing to many beliefs simultaneously.

The following phrases will help you join the discussion at religious or business meetings.

BUDDHISM			
Why does the lotus bloom?	*Hasu no hana ga saku, sono imi wa ikani?*	ハスの花が咲く、その意味はいかに？	*Ha-soo no HA-na ga SA-koo so-no EE-mee wa ee-CON-ee?*
What is the meaning of my bellybutton?	*Ohesotte nani?*	おへソって何？	*Oh-hay-so-tay nah-NEE?*
Where does all the money go?	*Kono okane wa donaru no desuka?*	このお金はどうなるのですか？	*KO-no oh-CON-ay wa doe-NAH-roo no DESK-ah?*

CULTURE 🔖

SHINTO

Always be sure to please the gods.	*Itsumo kamigami no ini shitagau—beshi.*	いつも神々の意に従うべし。	*ITS-mo KAH-me-GA-mee no EE-nee shee-TAG-ah oo-BESH-ee.*
When you have time.	*Sonna hima ga attara ne.*	そんな暇があったらね。	*So-nah HEE-ma ga AH-tah-rah nay.*
If you believe or not.	*Shinjite iyoto, shinjite imaito.*	信じていようと、信じていまいと。	*Shin-JEE-teh ee-YO-toh, shin-Jee-teh EE-ma-EE-toh.*

LIFO

Catch up and pass (the West)!	*Oitsuke oikose (seiyo ni)!*	追いつけ、追いこせ（西洋に）！	*Oh-eet-SOO-kay oh-ee-KO-say (SAY-oh nee)!*
Forget your wife and children.	*Tsuma ya kodomo o wasure nasai.*	妻や子供を忘れなさい。	*Tsoo-ma ya ko-DOH-mo oh wa-soo-ray na-SIGH.*
Follow the hierarchy or get squashed like the October plum.	*Soshiki ni shitagawa naito, umeboshi mitai ni hosareru yo.*	組織に従がわないと、梅干しみたいに干されるよ。	*So-SHEE-kee nee shee-tah-GA-wah na-EE-toh, oo-may-BOH-shee me-TAI nee HOH-sah-RAY-roo yoh.*

FIFO

Make GNP swell like belly of your wife!	*Anta no okusan no onaka mitaini GNP o fukurama se yo!*	あんたの奥さんのお腹みたいにGNPをふくらませよう！	*AHN-ta no OAK-san meet-ah-EE-nee gee en pee oh foo-koo RA-ma say yo!*
Make production flow like a mountain stream.	*Nagareru keiryu no yoni mono o seisan shitsuzukeyo.*	流れる渓流の様に物を生産し続けよう。	*Nah-ga-RAY-roo KAY-roo no YOH-nee MOH-no o say-san sheet-soo-zoo-KAY-oh.*
Vacation is for hooligans and foreigners soft as sashimi.	*Kyuka wa namakemono to sashimi mitaini yawana gaijin no kangaeru koto da.*	休暇はナマケ者と刺身みたいにやわな外人の考える事だ。	*Key-OO-kah wah NA-ma-kay-MOH-no toh sa-SHEE-mee MEET-ah-EE-nee ya-WAH-nah GUY-jeen no KON-gah-AY-roo KOH-toh da.*

QUOTE THE MASTERS

The Japanese love pithy sayings and seem to have one for every occasion. The most ancient of these sayings are Chinese, reflecting Japan's real philosophical heritage. Conversationalists should have a few aphorisms memorized to make points and conclude discussions.

	CONFUCIUS (551–479 B.C.)		
Four words the Master forbids: *certainly, shall, must* **and** *I.*	*Yottsu no kinku: kakujitsuni, zettai, nebanaranai, watashiga.*	四つの 禁句 ―確実に、 絶対、 ねばならない、 私が。	*YOTE-soo no KEEN-koo: KAH-koo-jeet-soo-nee zet-TAI, NAY-bah-NAH-rah-NAI, WAH-tah-SHEE-gah.*
Four words the Master likes very much: **perhaps, maybe, possibly and later.**	*Yottsu no yoi kotoba: moshikashite, tabun, kamoshirenai, atode.*	四つの良い 言葉 ―もし かして、 多分、かもし れない、 あとで。	*YOTE-soo no yoy KOH-toh-BAH: MOSH-kah-shee-TEH, tah-BUN, KAH-moh-SHEE-ren-AI, ah-TOE-day.*
The proper man understands equity; the small man, profit.	*Seijin wa kohei o aishi, bonjin wa rieki o aisu.*	聖人は公平 を愛し、凡人 は利益を 愛す。	*SAY-jeen wa KOH-high oh ah-EE-shee; BON-jeen wa ree-AY-kee oh ah-soo.*

| A nation of small men make a hell of a lot of profit. | *Bonjin bakari no kuni wa, rieki o takusan umu.* | 凡人ばかり の国は、 利益を たくさん産む。 | *BON-jeen bah-KAH-ree no koo-nee wa, ree-AY-kee oh TAH-koo-SAHN OO-moo* |

MENG-TSE (372–289? B.C.)

| He who drives well but putts poorly is like a brutish animal. | *Doraibu wa yoikedo patto ga hetana hito wa araarashii yaju to onaji da.* | ドライブは 良いけど パットが下手 な人は、 荒々しい野獣 と同じだ。 | *Doh-RAI-boo wa YOH-ee-kay-DOH PAH-toh ga hay-TAH-nah HEE-toh wa ah-RAH-rah-SHEE yah-joo toh oh-NAH-jee dah.* |

| He who putts well but drives poorly loses many balls. | *Patto wa yoiga doraibu ga hetana hito wa ushinau boru ga oi.* | パットは 良いが ドライブが 下手な人は 失なう ボールが 多い。 | *PAH-toh wa yoh-EE-gah doh-RAI-boo ga hay-TAH-nah HEE-toh wa OO-shee-now BOH-roo ga OH-ee.* |

| He who drives poorly and putts poorly should take up ikebana (flower arranging). | *Doraibu mo patto mo hetana hitoniwa ikebana ga aru.* | ドライブも パットも 下手な人 には活花があ る。 | *Doh-RAI-boo mo PAH-toh mo hay-TAH-nah HEE-toh-NEE-wah ee-KAY-bah-nah ga AH-roo* |

FOR WOMEN ONLY

In Japan as elsewhere, relations between the sexes are complex. Many of the same men who treat women as subhumans give their paychecks to their wives, who make all spending decisions.

Men's unpleasant attitudes are most likely to surface after three or four dozen drinks. They may try to hold an unfamiliar woman's hand in a bar or make rude comments while staggering through the streets. A pointed rebuke or two will usually stun them into more appropriate behavior.

That is not proper behavior where I come from.	*Watashi no kuni dewa souiumane wa shima sen.*	私の国では そういう 真似は しません。	*Wah-TASH-ee no koo-nee DAY-wah so-you-MAH-nay wa shee-MA-sen.*
Shame on you!	*Haji o shiri nasai!*	恥を知り なさい！	*HA-jee oh SHEE-ree nah-SIGH!*
Keep your hands to yourself.	*Te o shimai nasai.*	手をしまい なさい。	*Tay oh shee-MY nah-SIGH.*
If you want to keep all of your fingers.	*Otonashiku shinaito yubi o chongiru wayo.*	おとなしく しないと 指をちょん 切るわよ。	*OH-toh-na-SHEE-koo SHEE-nah-EE-toh Yoo-bee oh chong-EE-roo WHY-oh.*

You cold, raw fish without rice!	*Sashimi yaro!*	さしみ野郎！	*Sah-SHEE-me YAH-roh!*
Get ready to meet your ashamed ancestors!	*Anata no gosenzo sama ni kao o awase rare masuka!*	あなたの御先祖様に顔を合わせられますか！	*Ah-NAH-ta no goh-SEN-zoh SAH-ma ne kah-OH oh ah-WAH-say RAH-ray mah-soo-kah!*
You'd be no more than a snack for me.	*Hashi nimo bo nimo kakara nai wane!*	はしにも棒にもかからないわね。	*Hah-shee NEE-moh boh NEE-moh kah-KA-rah nai WAH-nay!*
I'll tear you in half!	*Mapputatsuni hiki sakuwayo!*	まっぷたつに引き裂くわよ！	*Mah-poo-TOT-soo-nay HEE-kee SAH-koo-WHY-oh!*

OH, NOH!

As one theatergoer put it, attending a *Noh* play is like being bitten to death by butterflies. The costumes and masks may be fantastic, the stories may be lurid, but the drama disappeared from *Noh* about a thousand years ago.

If you are forced to attend a *Noh* play, try to think of it as meditation rather than punishment. Your invitation to the theater is an honor, and you should be ready to comment on what you have seen.

That was different.	*Sozo ijo no mono deshita.*	想像以上の ものでした。	*Soh-zoh ee-joe no mono desh-tah.*
It was like drops of water boring a hole in my forehead.	*Suiteki de atama ni anao akerarete iru yona kokoromochi deshita.*	水滴で頭に 穴をあけら れている 様な心持ち でした。	*Soo-ee-TEK-ee day ah-TAH-ma nee ah-NAH-oh AH-kay-ra-RAY-tay EE-roo yoh-na KOH-koh roh-MOH-chee DESH-tah.*
I loved the part where the whole family disemboweled themselves.	*Kazoku sorrote no seppuku ga yokatta.*	家族そろって の切腹が よかった。	*Kah-ZOH-koo soh-ROH-teh no say-POO-koo ga yoh-KAH-tah.*

How sublime was their suffering!	*Karera no kurushimi wa nante totoi mono datta desho!*	彼らの苦しみは何て尊いものだったでしょう！	*Kah-RAY-rah no koo-roo-SHEE-mee wah NON-tay TOH-toy MOH-noh DAH-tah DAY-sho!*
How gracefully their guts fell to the floor!	*Harawata no kobore guai ni hin ga atta!*	腹ワタのこぼれ具合に品があった！	*HAH-rah-WAH-tah no koh-BOH-ray goo-AI nee heen ga AH-tah!*
Their deaths perfectly expressed my deepest desires.	*Watashi no nozomi dori no shinikata deshita ne.*	私の望みどおりの死に方でしたね。	*Wah-TAH-shee no noh-ZOH-mee DOH-ree noh SHEE-nee-KAH-tah DESH-tah nay.*

CULTURE 🪷

THE SUTRA ON THE EIGHT REALIZATIONS FOR THE 1990s

For more than 2000 years, Buddhists have meditated on the Eight Realizations of the Sutra to escape the cycles of birth and death known as *samsara* and achieve the peace known as *nirvana*.

As Japanese society advances, the Sutra is modified to suit the times.

ANCIENT REALIZATION	MODERN REALIZATION
All material things are impermanent.	Every warranty must eventually expire.
Desires lead only to more desires.	Who owns a compact disk player must purchase compact disks.
Laziness is an obstacle to perfection.	Vacation leads to poor quality control.
Ignorance results in endless rounds of death and rebirth.	Attend top university or face eternal shame.
Poverty leads to anger and hatred.	A homogeneous middle-class society is a peaceful one.
Avoid all worldly distractions.	Ignore the suffering of non-Japanese people.
Help others find the path to joy.	Lend money and sell high-quality products to every person on earth.

JAPANESE ROADSIGNS

If you must drive in Japan, be sure to familiarize yourself with the unique local roadsigns.

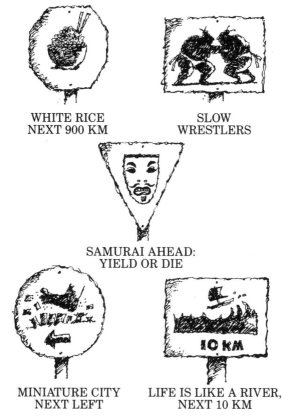

WHITE RICE
NEXT 900 KM

SLOW
WRESTLERS

SAMURAI AHEAD:
YIELD OR DIE

MINIATURE CITY
NEXT LEFT

LIFE IS LIKE A RIVER,
NEXT 10 KM

THE CROWDED SUBWAY, JUDO AND YOU

Japanese subways are fast, efficient and convenient. They can also be extraordinarily crowded. White-gloved "pushers" will kindly shove you into a rush-hour train.

Japanese *en route* can be extremely rude. They have a saying: "*Tabi no haji wa kakisute,*" or "The traveler's shame can be brushed off." New York subways seem almost genteel compared to those in Japan.

Men shove old ladies aside for seats, and you're sure to be knocked around by people heading for the door. Women may find unwelcome body parts pressed against them. A few phrases, combined with proper judo strikes, may help you vent some of your frustration.

INSULT	JUDO RESPONSE	VERBAL ASSAULT	JAPANESE
Reading paper in your face.	Silent meditation: "May Death Come Soon to Infidels."	None	
Falling fast asleep, using you as mattress.	Wet willie-san (moistened finger poked into enemy ear).	"Good morning!"	おはよう！ **Ohayo!** *Oh-HI-oh!*
Strong shove.	Grab opponent's suit coat side pocket. Rip downwards, firmly.	"So sorry."	ゴメンナサイ、 **Gomennasai.** *Go-MEN-nah-SIGH.*
Lascivious rubbing.	Strike firmly at tender organs.	"Police! Arrest this pervert!"	おまわりさん！痴漢をつかまえて！ **Omawarisan! Chikan o tsukamaete!** *Oh-MAH-wah-ree-san! Chee-KAN oh TSKA-mah-teh!*

ZEN CAB: WHAT IS FINAL DESTINATION OF MOTIONLESS TAXI?

Like almost everything else in Japan, taxis are new, expensive and spotless. The fares are so high that you half-expect the drivers to speak a little English and serve drinks.

They may wear white gloves, but *untenshu-san* won't speak your language. They can't read your mind, either. Explaining where you want to go is complicated by the fact that few streets have names and building numbers are chosen according to the whims of several especially cruel Shinto gods.

Ask your host or concierge to write directions to your destination on a slip of paper for your driver, and have about three thousand yen—in cash—for your fare.

| This is where I am going. | *Koko e itte kudasai.* | ここへ行って下さい。 | *KOH-koh eh EE-tay koo-dah-SIGH.* |

Could we be there in two hours?	*Ni-jikan de tsukimasuka?*	２時間で着きますか？	*Nee-jee-KAHN day tsoo-KEE-mah-SKA?*
In time for the next vernal equinox, then?	*Rainen no shunbun madeniwa tsukimasuyone?*	来年の春分までには着きますよね？	*RYE-nen no SHUN-bun mah-day-NEE-wa TSOO-kee-mah-soo-YOH-nay?*
Say, this is an impressive traffic jam!	*Nante komikata nandesho!*	なんて混み方なんでしょ！	*NON-tay koh-mee-KAH-tah nan-DAY-sho!*
We haven't moved a millimeter in half an hour.	*San-ju punkan ichi-miri mo susunde inai.*	30分間１ミリも進んでいない。	*SAHN-joo poon-kan EE-chee-MEE-ree mo soo-SUN-day ee-NIGH.*
Sir, I think you are too polite.	*Moshi moshi, anata wa hikaeme sugimasenka.*	もしもし、あなたは控目すぎませんか。	*Moosh moosh, ah-NAH-tah wa HEE-ka-AY-may soo-gee-ma-SEN-ka.*
Do you mind if I honk?	*Watashi ni kurakushon osasete moraemasuka?*	私にクラクション押させてもらえますか？	*Wah-TAH-shee nee koo-RAK-shon OH-sah-SAY-tay MOH-rah-ay-MOSS-ka?*

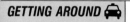

EMERGENCIES

Disorder is rare in Japan, but in case of emergency, dialing 110 will reach the police and 119 an ambulance or fire crew. No one who answers will speak English, however, so you need to be prepared with a couple of key phrases.

Emergency!	*Tasukete oisogi!*	たすけて、大急ぎ！	*Tah-soo-KAY-tay OH-ee-SOH-ghee!*
I am at the corner of two nameless streets!	*Nanashi no nihon no michi no kado ni imasu!*	名無しの二本の道の角にいます！	*NAH-nah-SHEE no NEE-hone no MEE-chee no KAH-doh nee ee-MOSS!*
I am near a sushi bar/ electronics store/ boutique!	*Sushiya/ denkiya/ buttiku no soba desu!*	寿司屋／電器屋／ブティックのそばです！	*Soo-SHEE-ah/den-KEE-ya/boo-tee-koo no so-ba DAY-soo!*
I need an ambulance/ fire truck/ policeman/ large cash advance!	*Kyukyusha/ shobosha/ omawarisan/ tairyo no genkin no maegari ga imasugu hitsuyo nanda!*	救急車／消防車／おまわりさん／大量の現金の前措りが今すぐ必要なんだ！	*Kee-yoo-kee-yoo-sha/SHO-bo-sha/oh-MA-wa-ree-san/TIE-ree-oh no GHEN-keen no ma-AY-ga-ree ga ee-ma-SOO-goo HEET-soo-YOH NON-dah!*

🌀 ENTERTAINMENT AND OBSESSION

PLAY-BY-PLAY SUMO

Sumo (pronounced "smo"), fat-power wrestling, is over a thousand years old. Wrestlers stomp their feet, clap their hands, throw salt and lift their fat eyelids to glare at each other.

A little knowledgeable commentary will give you more prestige in the eyes of your hosts.

What a mighty mountain of meat!	*Nante okina niku no katamari desho!*	なんて 大きな肉の かたまりで しょう！	*NON-tay OH-keen-ah NEE-koo no KA-ta-MA-ree day-SHO!*
He looks as grand and immobile as Mount Fuji.	*Okikute ugokasenai fuji-san mitai da.*	大きくて 動かせない 富士山 みたいだ。	*Oh-KEE-koo-tay OO-go-ka-SEN-ai FOO-ji-san mee-TAI da.*
Whoops! He isn't as imposing flat on his back, is he?	*Are! Taoreteruto sonnani osoroshikumo naina?*	あれ！倒れて ると そんなに 恐しくも ないなあ？	*Ah-RAY! TAH-ray-tay-ROO-toh so-NAH-nee oh-so-ROSH-koo-mo na-ee-NAH?*

BARBARIC BASEBALL CHEERS

Corporate life is so pervasive that even *beisu-boru* teams represent giant corporations, not cities or regions. And whether they're on the job or at a ball game, the Japanese are comfortable taking orders and preserving harmony.

Fans, even the most rabid, usually remain silent and motionless until professional cheerleaders tell them to make a team cheer or sing a team song. Amaze fans and players by being the only person among thousands to yell insults at the top of your lungs.

Hey batter batter!	*Ohi batta batta!*	オーイ バッター バッター！	*OH-ee bah-TAH bah-TAH!*
Stand up, little fellow!	*Chikkoino, okiagareyo!*	ちっこいの、起きあがれよ！	*CHEE-koh-EE-noh, oh-KEE-ah-gah-RAY-oh!*
Easy out! Easy out!	*Kantan! Kantan!*	かんたん！ かんたん！	*Kahn-TAHN! Kahn-TAHN!*
Aw! My mother has a better swing!	*Ah, uchi no kachan no ho ga ee battingu suruyo!*	アー、うちの母ちゃんの方がいいバッティングするよ！	*Ah, OO-chee no KAH-chan no ho ga ay bah-TEEN-goo soo-roo-yo!*

🎾 ENTERTAINMENT AND OBSESSION

Where's your makeup, you geisha!	*Okesho wa doshitano, geisha-san!*	お化粧は どうしたの、 芸者さん！	*Oh-KESH-oh wa DOSH-tah-no GAY-sha-sahn!*
Shame! Public humiliation!	*Ahoka! Sodai gomi!*	あほか！ 粗大ゴミ！	*Ah-ho-ka! SO-dai go-mee!*
Forget baseball!	*Yakyu, yame chimae!*	野球やめ ちまえ！	*YAK-ee-yoo, YAH-may chee-MAI!*
Go get us some tea!	*Ocha kunde koi!*	お茶くんで こい！	*Oh-CHA kund-eh-KOY!*

AUTHENTIC BASEBALL CHEERS

O fighting spirit! Fly, fireball, into the sky!
O Giants with honorable diamond Playing strong!
Giants! Giants! Go! Go! Heroes!

Storm clouds penetrated! By balls to the star of victory!
O Giants with honorable name—tomorrow!
Grow! Our team! Brave and heroic!
Giants! Giants! Go! Go! Heroes!

GOLF AS WAR

Membership in a top Japanese country club now costs over a million dollars. Serious golfers are therefore every bit as elite today as the samurai were in feudal times.

Like sword-fighting, *gorufu* suits the Japanese taste for Zen—the harder one tries, the worse one plays.

The Japanese also like activities that require special clothes. They purchase extravagant golf wardrobes and look extremely silly.

If you are invited to play a round in Japan, never fear. Your opponents may adopt samurai spirit and attempt to cut you to ribbons, but they can't play worth spit.

What are the stakes here?	*Kakekin wa ikura desuka?*	かけ金は いくら ですか？	*KAH-kay-kin wa ee-koo-rah DESK-ah?*
A bottle of sake per hole? Done.	*Pahoru goto osake ippon? Kekko desu ne.*	パーホール ごと、お酒 1本？ 結構です ね。	*Pa-HO-roo GO-toh oh-SAH-kay ee-PON? KEK-oh DAY-soo nay.*
Well done! That was a long drive for a man your size.	*Yatta! Karada no wari ni yoku tobi mashita ne.*	やった！ 体の割りに よく飛び ましたね。	*Ya-TAH! Kah-RA-da no WAH-ree nee YOH-koo TOH-bee MOSH-tah nay.*

🌀 ENTERTAINMENT AND OBSESSION

Ah! Bad luck, Suzuki-san!	*Ah, un ga warui ne, suzuki-san!*	アー、運が悪いね、鈴木さん！	*Ah, uhn ga wah-ROO-ee-nay, soo-ZOO-kee-san!*
Only a meter short of the green!	*Gurin ni ichi metoru tarinai!*	グリーンに１メートル足りない！	*Goo-REEN nee EE-chee MAY-toh-roo TAH-ree-nigh!*
And such a deep bunker, too.	*Soreni nante hidoi banka nan desho.*	それに何てひどいバンカーなんでしょ。	*Soh-REN-ee NON-tay hee-DOY bahn-KA non DAY-sho.*
You'll need a ladder to get down into that one.	*Oriru noni hashigo ga iru to omoimasu.*	おりるのにハシゴがいると思います。	*Oh-REE-roo NOH-nee ha-SHEE-go ga EE-roo toh oh-MO-ee-MOSS.*
Would you like to borrow my excellent sand wedge?	*Watashi no jotona sandowejji o okashi shimashoka?*	私の上等なサンドウェッジをお貸ししましょうか？	*Wah-TAH-shee no jo-TOH-nah SAN-doh-WEH-jee oh oh-KOSH-ee SHEE-ma-SHOH-ka?*

DEFENSIVE DRIVING

Gorufu is so popular that some people practice for years without getting onto a course. They will swing umbrellas, rolled-up newspapers and "air clubs," anything to display their good taste.

The closest they may get to actual golf is at cavernous, multistory driving ranges. If you'd like to hit balls at a Japanese driving range, you'll need a few phrases.

A big bucket of balls, please.	*Okina baketsu ippai no boru, onegai shimasu.*	大きなバケツ１杯のボール、お願いします。	*OH-key-nah bah-KET-soo ee-PIE no bo-roo, oh-nay-GUY shee-MOSS.*
Do you have anything near the ground floor?	*Jimen ni chikai tokoro arimasuka?*	地面に近いところありますか？	*JEE-men nee chee-KAI toh-KOH-roh ah-ree-MOSS-kah?*
I'm looking for a sense of realism.	*Jissaidori ni yaritain desu.*	実際通りにやりたいんです。	*Jee-SAI-doh-ree nee yar-ee-TINE DAY-soo.*
Do you also rent helmets?	*Herumetto mo arimasuka?*	ヘルメットもありますか？	*Hay-roo-MAY-toh mo AR-ee-MOSS-ka?*
The other golfers look a little wild tonight.	*Konya wa minna aretemasune.*	今夜はみんな荒れてますね。	*KOH-nee-ah wa MEE-nah ah-RAY-tay-MOSS-nay.*

CEREMONY OF THE BON BON

Those who violate the stark rules of gift-giving may be tatooed as boors forever. To achieve the rank of Gift Master you must follow these rules:

Wait for them to give. If you present your hosts with chocolate and they have none for you, your bon bons will be received as small brown insults. By tradition, the recipients will be compelled to destroy you.

Don't be cheap or extravagant. A briefcase full of unmarked bills is as embarrassing as a Budweiser T-shirt. The recipient is likely to respond with a series of firm kicks to your head and midriff.

Do not give gifts in multiples of four. The number four means death to the Japanese. An equivalent gift in the United States is a dead fish.

Wrap carefully in Japanese rice paper, the most important part of the gift. Content is less important than form. As you reach the level of Gift Master, your need to give and receive actual gifts will gradually disappear. A hollow box of rice paper will be enough.

STRAW BED & RAW BREAKFAST

Travelers can get a taste of traditional Japan by staying in a *ryokan* (guest house).

If you are successful in obtaining a reservation, remove your shoes upon entering the hotel. Your maid will lead you to your room; do not step on the tatami mats. Guests take communal baths before dinner is served in their rooms.

What pleasant furnishings!	*Nante suteki na oheya desho!*	なんてすてきなお部屋でしょう！	*NON-tay STEK-ee na oh-HAY-ah day-SHO!*
A table and two cushions!	*Teiburu to nimai no zabuton!*	テーブルと二枚のざぶとん！	*TAY-boo-roo toh NEE-mai no ZAH-boo-TOHN!*
Hey, who needs a chair/sofa/bed/TV anyway?	*Choto, isu/ sofa/beddo/ terebi nante iranaiyone?*	ちょっと、イス / ソファ /ベッド / テレビなんていらないよね？	*CHOH-toh, EE-soo/so-FA/ BED-oh/tay-RAY-bee NON-tay ee-rah-NAI-oh-neh?*
Madam, please change the sheet on my futon.	*Okami san, futon no shitsu o kaete kudasai.*	おかみさん、フトンのシーツをかえて下さい。	*Oh-KAH-me sahn, FOO-ton no SHEET-soo oh ka-AY-tay koo-dah-SIGH.*

It smells of pickled eel.	*Unagi no tsukemono mitaina nioi da.*	うなぎの漬物みたいな匂いだ。	*Oo-NAH-ghee no TSOO-kay-moh-noh MEE-tah-EE-nah nee-OH-ee da.*
One more thing—would you bring me toast and coffee for breakfast.	*Eto sorekara—tosuto to kohi no choshoku arimasuka.*	エート、それから…。トーストとコーヒーの朝食ありますか。	*AY-toh so-RAY-ka-RA—TOAST-oh toh KOH-HEE no CHOASH-koo AR-ee-MOSS-kah.*
No rice. No fish. No raw egg. Please.	*No gohan. No sushi. No nama tamago. Onegai shimasu.*	ノーごはん、ノーすし、ノー生卵、お願いします。	*No go-HAHN. No SOO-shee. No NAH-ma tah-MA-go. OH-nay-GUY shee-MOSS.*
I am too barbaric to eat a Japanese breakfast.	*Nihonshoku o tabetsukete inai yabanjin desu.*	日本食を食べつけていない野蛮人です。	*NEE-hone-SHO-koo oh TAH-bay-soo-KAY-tay ee-NAI YA-bon-JEEN DAY-soo.*

WISE LOSS OF FACE

Some Japanese bars take advantage of cultural taboos by not listing prices; men consider it shameful to ask about price before ordering. This can be hazardous for those not flying on company plastic—a couple of rounds of drinks may cost hundreds of dollars. Some establishments, known as *boryoku* bars (violence bars), employ karate experts to extract payment from balky customers.

If you do ask about prices, try to do so privately, as your Japanese guests will be ashamed by your queries and will never go out with you again.

How much is whiskey/beer/ sake?	*Uisuki/biru/ sake wa ikura desuka?*	ウイスキー /ビール / 酒はいく らですか？	*OO-ee-soo- KEE/BEE- roo/SAH-kay wah ee-koo- rah DESK- ah?*
Thirty dollars each?	*Ippai, yonsen gohyaku en?*	1杯、四千 五百円？	*Ee-PAI, YON- sen GO-hee- AH-koo en?*
What do we get with our drinks?	*Ippai ni tsuki nani ga tsuite kuruno?*	1杯につき 何がつい てくるの？	*Ee-PAI nee TSOO-key NAH-nee ga TSO-ee-tay koo-loo-noh?*

Polar ice and silk napkins?	*Nankyoku no kori to kinu no napukin demo kuruno?*	南極の氷と絹のナプキンでもくるの？	*NANK-oh-koo no KOH-ree toh KEE-noo no NAP-oo-kin DAY-mo KOO-roo-no?*
And a little respect from a bartender?	*Batensan no okini sawari mashitaka?*	バーテンさんのお気にさわりましたか？	*BAH-ten-sahn no oh-KEE-nee sah-WAH-ree MOSH-tock-ah?*

RENT-A-COFFIN

Kapuseru hoteru (capsule hotels) were designed for two sorts of customers: men who miss their trains and vampires on tight budgets. "Rooms" are divided into large coffins, stacked three high and made of plastic for easy cleaning. *Totemo benri!* (How convenient!) Naturally, each coffin is equipped with a mattress and TV.

Kapuseru hoteru can be found near almost any large train station, but they are not recommended for people of normal size. If you are forced to stay in one, remember, don't wear shoes in your windowless plastic cubbyhole! That would be uncivilized!

VISITING THE JAPANESE HOME

The Japanese entertain at home about as often as we entertain in our closets, but if you do visit a private home, be ready with a few compliments.

Your garden is like a jewel.	*Hoseki no yona niwa desune.*	宝石のような庭ですね。	*HO-sek-ee no yo-nah NEE-wa DAY-soo-nay.*
As the breeze flows through the shrub, my heart is at peace.	*Midori o nukeru soyokaze ga, watashi no kokoro o nagomasete kure masu.*	緑をぬけるそよ風が、私の心をなごませてくれます。	*Mee-DOH-ree oh noo-KAY-roo SOY-oh-KAW-zay gah, wa-TAH-shee no koh-KOH-roh oh NAH-go-MAH-say-tay KOO-ray moss.*
The stone in the pond is as fluid and elegant as a mythical bird.	*Ike no ishi wa shinwa no tori no yoni yuga de furyu desu.*	池の石は神話の鳥のように優雅で風流です。	*EE-kay no EE-shee wa SHEEN-wa no TOH-ree no YOH-nee YOO-ga day FOOR-yoo DAY-soo.*
And in the living room, I am struck by the Hello Kitty motif.	*Ima no kitty-chan no kazaritsuke niwa kando shimashita.*	居間のキティちゃんの飾りつけには感動しました。	*EE-ma no KEE-tee-chan no ka-zah-REET-soo-kay NEE-wa kan-DOH shee-MOSH-tah.*

DINING ETIQUETTE FOR BARBARIANS

While Japan has one of the most formal cultures ever invented, some of its customs make perfect sense. We all know that shoes are dirty things, for example; in Japan they are removed before entering a home or *zashiki* (a private room in a restaurant). On a trip to the *toile*, you must change into special rubber slippers. Failure to do so will win you the social standing of a sewer rat.

When using chopsticks **never**:

- Use them to pass food to someone else. This is how the bones of dead family members are handled by Buddhist priests;

- Stick them vertically into the rice. This turns the meal into an offering for the dead;

- Lick them unless you want to take your fellow diners to bed;

- Display your grasp of Zen by trying to catch flies with your chopsticks. It's much harder than it looks.

HONORABLE TEA

Coffee (*kohi*) is becoming more popular, but honorable tea (*o-cha*) remains as essential to Japanese life as rice and microchips. In offices and homes, tea is served at ten o'clock in the morning and again at three in the afternoon.

The ideal green tea is clear, bitter and still boiling when it hits the roof of your mouth. It is potent: one cup is usually enough to get an unconscious reveler out of the gutter and on his way to work with a smile on his face and a pulse of 160.

Honorable tea? Yes, please!	*Ocha? Hai, onegai shimasu.*	お茶？はい、お願いします！	*Oh-CHA? Hai, OH-nay-GUY shee-MOSS.*
I drank some after I got off the plane last week.	*Senshu hikoki kara orite ippai nomimashita.*	先週、飛行機から降りて1杯飲みました。	*San-SHOO hee-KOH-kee KA-rah oh-REE-tay ee-PAI noh-min-MOSH-tah.*
I haven't slept since.	*Sore irai neteimasen.*	それ以来寝ていません。	*SO-ray ee-RAI nay-TAY-ee-MOSS-en.*
I have many evil thoughts.	*Osoroshii kangae nimo osoware masu.*	恐ろしい考えにも襲われます。	*OH-so-ROH-shee kahn-GAY NEE-moh OH-so-WA-ray MOSS.*

In short, I love green tea.	*Demo kekkyoku, watashi wa ocha ga sukidesu.*	でも結局、私はお茶が好きです。	*DAY-moh cake-YOH-koo, wa-TOSH-ee wa oh-CHA ga soo-key-DAY-soo.*
Do you know where I could find a nickel bag of the stuff?	*Nikkeru-bag wa dokode teni hairi masuka?*	ニッケルバッグは、どこで手に入りますか？	*NEE-kay-roo-bag wah DOH-koh-DAY ten-EE ha-EE-ree MOSS-ka?*

SAKE TO ME

Sake is not just a drink: it is a holy sacrament of conversation, meditation and oblivion. Thus there are special rules regarding its use.

Don't let anyone's sake cup become empty. And don't drink the last few drops from your cup; wait until it is refilled.

When sake is poured, take a sip immediately. It will be boiling hot, but you must not lose face. You can seek medical attention later.

As your vision and speech begin to blur, try not to throw up or ridicule anyone's haircut. Shots of hot tea may revive you enough to keep drinking.

AVOIDING AMBULATORY FOOD

There are two things to watch out for in Japanese restaurants: prices and food. If prices aren't marked on the menu, beware—your meal may cost more than a piece of Tokyo real estate. The food, meanwhile, will be anxious and upset—keep fingers, hair, and clothing away from the animals on the table.

That looks good.	*Yosasou desune.*	良さそう です ね。	*YO-sah-so dess-NAY.*
Please tie it down/cook it.	*Osaete kudasai/ryori shite.*	おさえて 下さい / 料理して。	*OH-sah-ay-TAY koo-DA-sai ree-OH-ree shee-TAY.*
The broth is for drowning?	*Kono dashijiru de oboresaseru no desuka?*	このダシ汁 でおぼれ させるの ですか？	*Koh-NOH DAH-shee-JEE-roo day OH-boh-RAY-sah-SAY-roo no DESK-ah?*
How the honorable shrimp struggle as they choke to death!	*Ebi no idaina saigo desu!*	エビの 偉大な最期 です！	*Eh-BEE no ee-DAI-nah sai-GO DAY-soo!*

Do you serve any completely dead domestic animals?	*Ugoki dasanai kachiku no niku, arimasenka?*	動き出さない家畜の肉、ありませんか？	*Oo-GO-kee DA-sah-NAI KA-chee-KOO noh nee-KOO, ah-REE-mah-SEN-KA?*
How about some fried/boiled beef?	*Sukiyaki/shabu-shabu wa arimasuka?*	すきやき／シャブシャブはありますか？	*Skee-YA-kee shah-BOO-shah-BOO wa AH-ree-MOSS-ka?*
Great. Bring me some ketchup/Coke with that, please.	*Yokatta. Kechappu/kora mo kudasai.*	よかった。ケチャップ／コーラも下さい。	*Yoh-KAH-TAH. KAY-chah-poo/koh-rah mo KOO-DA-sai.*

FUGU ROULETTE

Fugu is blowfish, prepared by highly-trained chefs who remove most—but not all—of the fish's deadly poison. Chefs do make mistakes, of course, but that's what makes fugu so exciting.

No, please. After you.	*Iie, dozo. Osakini.*	いいえ。 どうぞお先に。	*EE-ay, DOH-zoh, OH-sah-KEE-nee.*
I hate to disturb the artwork of the chef.	*Shefu no geijutsu sakuhin o kowashitaku nai.*	シェフの 芸術作品を こわしたく ない。	*SHEF-oo no guy-JOOT-soo SAK-oo-HEEN oh koh-WAH-shee-TOK nai.*
Well, how is it?	*Sate, Dodesuka?*	さて、どう ですか？	*SAH-tay, DOH-desk?*
You look okay.	*Daijobusou desune.*	大丈夫そう ですね。	*Dai-JO-boo-soo dess-NAY.*
What the hell, I'll have some.	*Konattara, watashi mo itadakimasho.*	こうなった ら、私も いただきま しょう。	*KOH-nah-tah-rah, wah-TOSH mo ee-TAH-dah-kee-imosh-OH.*
Hey, you're eating my share!	*Chotto, watashi no bun mo tabeteru!*	ちょっと 私の分も 食べてる！	*CHO-toh, wah-TOSH no boon moh TAH-bay-TAY-roo!*

SLURP AS BUDDHA

Like each stone in a pond, each slurp in a meal represents a chance to touch perfection. But different slurps are required for different dishes, just as each stone has its own place.

Soup is slurped gently but firmly. Eyes are directed skyward, not to the bowl, as this would make the diner appear cross-eyed. This soup-slurp is known as "Praying Mantis Style."

The long noodle is slurped without regard for launched vegetables or flung broth. The steady flowing motion, much like the smooth tongue-flicking of a small aardvark in the autumn moonlight inspires the name, "Esteemed Ant-Eater Method."

The slice of boiled pork is slurped while offering silent thanks to the spirit of the departed pig for its contribution to the meal. The master diner simply pokes his or her face into the bowl. Once the pork is grasped, the head is thrown back and the slice inhaled so quickly that the motion is invisible to the Western eye. This is known as the "Wild-Dog-in-the-Alley Technique."

IMPRESSING YOUR GEISHA

You're not likely to meet any authentic geisha, but you probably will meet their less-well-trained counterparts known as *hosutesu*. Geisha and *hosutesu* are not prostitutes. They pride themselves on their refined charm and culture, so ambitious men do well to adopt a little of their own.

I am honored to meet you, miss.	*Oaidekite koeidesu, ojosama.*	お会いできて光栄です、お嬢様。	*OH-ai-DAY-kee-tay KOH-ai-DAY-soo, oh-JOH-sah-ma.*
You are as beautiful as spring's first cherry blossom.	*Anata wa haru ichiban no sakura no yoni utsukushii.*	あなたは春一番の桜の様に美しい。	*Ah-NAH-ta wa HA-roo EE-chee-bahn no sa-KOO-ra no YOH-nee OOTS-koo-shee.*
Read any good haiku lately?	*Haiku demo hitotsu dodesuka?*	俳句でも一つどうですか？	*HAI-koo DAY-mo hee-TOTE-soo doh-DESK-ah?*
Which poet is your favorite?	*Dare ga suki desuka?*	誰が好きですか？	*DAH-ray ga soo-kee DESK-ah?*
You recite wonderfully.	*Nante subarashii okoe desho.*	なんてすばらしい御声でしょう。	*NON-tay soo-ba-ROSH oh-KOH-ay day-SHO.*

But haiku is such a short form.	*Haiku wa mijikai desune.*	俳句は短いですね。	*HAI-koo wa MEE-jee-kai dess-NAY.*
I happen to have an epic poem with me.	*Subarashii shio motte kite imasu.*	すばらしい詩を持ってきています。	*Soo-ba-ROSH SHEE-oh MO-tay KEE-tay ee-MOSS.*
Come back to my hotel and let me show it to you.	*Hoteru ni itte issho ni yomi masenka.*	ホテルに行って一緒に読みませんか。	*Ho-TAY-roo nee EE-tay EE-sho nee YOH-mee ma-SEN-kah.*

SOCIAL JAPAN

GETTING NAKED IN JAPAN

As high-tech as Japan may seem, millions of Japanese homes have no plumbing. Many people go to *ofuroya* (public baths) to bathe and relax in communal tubs.

Everyone washes at basins before getting into the tubs. For filthy *gaijin,* this is especially important because bathwater is reused and regulars may be disgusted to share it with you. You can take advantage of their disgust, however, to get a whole tub to yourself.

Pardon me, but have you a bigger towel?	*Sumimasen, okina taoru arimasuka?*	すみません、大きなタオルありますか？	*SOO-mee-MA-sen, oh-KEE-nah tay-OH-roo AH-ree-MOSS-ka?*
I don't want to frighten anyone.	*Hokanohito o odokashi taku nai.*	他の人をおどかしたくない。	*Ho-KA-no-HEE-toh oh OH-doh-KA-shee TA-koo nai.*
Good evening. Is there room for me in this tub?	*Konbanwa. Watashi no hairu tokoro arimasuka?*	今晩は。私の入るところありますか？	*Kon-BAHN-wa. Wa-TA-shee no HI-roo toh-KOH-roh AH-ree-MOSS-ka?*
Ayee! Hot as molten lava!	*Atsui! Yogan mitai!*	熱い！溶岩みたい！	*Aht-soo-ee! Yo-GAHN mee-TAI!*

I like you.	*Anata ga sukidesu.*	あなたが好きです。	*Ah-NAH-tah ga SOO-key-DESS.*
Do you mind if I sit in your lap?	*Anata no hiza ni suwattemo yoroshii deshoka?*	あなたのヒザに坐ってもよろしいでしょうか？	*Ah-NAH-tah no HEE-za nee SOO-wa-TAY-mo yo-ROH-shee day-SHOKE?*
Please massage my thighs.	*Watashi no huto momo o monde kudasai.*	私の太モモをもんで下さい。	*Wah-TOSH no HOO-toh MOH-moh oh MONE-day KOO-dah-SIGH.*
Hey! Where's everybody going?	*Are! Minna doko ittano?*	あれ！みんなどこ行ったの？	*Ah-RAY! MEEN-ah DOH-ko ee-TAH-noh?*

THE KARAOKE BAR

Business associates go out in a group nearly every night. So profound is their boredom and so heavy is their drinking that they entertain each other by singing popular songs accompanied by taped music.

The Japanese enjoy "Love Me Tender" and "Home on the Range," but if you really want to make friends and influence people, serenade them with "Kimigayo."

KIMIGAYO			
May thy glorious, glorious reign Last for ages, myriad ages, Till the tiny pebbles small Into mighty rocks shall grow— Hoary moss shall overgrow them all.	*Kimi ga yo wa Chiyo ni yachiyo ni Sazare ishi no Iwao to narite—Koke no musu made.*	君が代は 千代に 八千代に 小石の 巌となりて 苔のむす まで	*KEE-mee ga yo wa CHEE-oh nee ya-CHEE-oh nee Sa-ZA-ray EE-shee no Ee-WAY-oh toh na-REE-tay—Ko-kay no MOO-soo MA-day.*

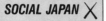

ALE BONDING

The Japanese tradition of fellowship with *na-kama* (business buddies) is called *otsukiai*. Drinking too much and acting like dirty little boys is a tradition among company men.

If you'd like to gain the trust of your associates, you must get so staggering drunk that you'll willingly pick up a microphone and serenade a barful of giggling men.

Cheers!	*Kampai!*	かんぱーい。	*Kam-PAI!*
Chug it!	*Ikki, ikki!*	一気、一気！	*Icky, icky!*
Bring us a whole bottle!	*Botoru ippon motte kite!*	ボトル1本もってきて！	*Boh-TOH-roo ee-PON MOH-tay KEE-tay!*
Hey Kazuko-san, you look a little green!	*Chotto kazukosan, aozameteruyo!*	ちょっとかず子さん、青ざめてるよ！	*CHOH-toh ka-ZOO-ko-san, ay-oh-ZA-may-tay-ROO-yoh!*
Get him a drink/ wheelchair/ doctor!	*Hayaku nomimono/ kurumaisu/ isha o kare ni!*	はやく、飲物／車イス／医者を彼に！	*Hah-YA-koo NO-mee-MO-no/koo-roo-MY-soo/ EESH-ah oh KA-ray nee!*
Hey, this is fun!	*Koitsua omoshiroiya!*	こいつあ、おもしろいや！	*Ko-eet-soo-ah OH-mo-shee-ROY-ah!*

"LIFE" IN A JAPANESE FIRM

To work for a Japanese company you must forget your Western ways. You will be expected to dedicate your body and soul to work. Nothing can take precedence over the needs of the corporation, including your own emotional or financial well-being. And the firm has no room for stars, mavericks or non-Japanese executives, no matter what their talents.

The following phrases will help you in job interviews. You may also use them as mantras in your effort to hypnotize yourself into wanting to work for a Japanese firm.

I want to sing the company song six mornings a week for the rest of my life.	*Shinumade, shu ni muika, maiasa shaka o utaitai to omoimasu.*	死ぬまで、週に6日、毎朝社歌を唄いたいと思います。	*SHEE-noo-MAH-day, shoo nee moo-EE-ka, my-AH-sah SHA-ka OO-tai-tai toh oh-MO-ee-*
I will always agree with my superiors, even when they are totally wrong.	*Tatoe karera ga machigatte itemo, watashi no joshi niwa sakarai masen.*	たとえ彼らがまちがっていても、私の上司には逆らいません。	*Ta-TOH ka-RAY-rah ga MAH-chee-GA-tay ee-TAY-mo, wa-TASH no JO-shee NEE-wa SA-ka-RAI MOSS-en.*

💼 WORKING FOR THE JAPANESE

I do not care about making money.	*Okanemoke ni kyomi wa arimasen.*	お金儲けに興味は有りません。	*Oh-KAH-nay-MO-kay nee kee-YOH-mee wa AH-ree-MOSS-en.*
My dream is to be a tiny cog in a huge and honorable machine.	*Yumei na daigaisha no hitotsu no haguruma ni naritai.*	有名な大会社の一つの歯車になりたい。	*YOO-may na dai-GAI-shah no hee-TOTE-soo no ha-GOO-roo-ma nee NA-ree-TAI.*
When my firm has no more use for me, I will go quietly to my death.	*Watashi ni yo ga nakunattara, sumiyakani hakaba e mairimasu.*	私に用がなくなったら、すみやかに墓場へまいります。	*Wa-TAH-shee nee yo ga nah-KOO-nah-tah-rah, SOO-mee-ah-KAH-nee ha-KAH-ba ay MAR-ee-MOSS.*

WORKING FOR THE JAPANESE 💼

COMPANY SONGS

Dedication to a corporation is so contrary to human nature that employees of Japanese firms must be subjected to daily hypnosis. The company song is an important part of this indoctrination.

The following song is a typical example. In order to remain happy in your job, insert the name of your firm in the song of your choice and sing it at least twice a day.

	O GLORIOUS CORPORATION! *IDAI NA KAISHA!*		
We find meaning of life at (company name)!	*Jinsei no ikigai o (kaisha mei) de mitsuketa!*	人生の生きがいを（社名）で見つけた！	*JIN-say no EE-kee-GAI oh (company name) day MEET-skay-tah!*
Real family is here in enormous office building!	*Kyodai biru no naka wa mina kazoku!*	巨大ビルの内は皆家族！	*Kai-oh-DAI BEE-roo no NAH-ka wa MEE-na KAZ-koo!*
We love our unity!	*Icchi danketsu shiyo!*	一致団結しよう！	*EE-chee dahn-KET-soo shee-YO!*
Ten thousand employees pressed tightly together.	*Ichi-mannin no nakama no katai kessoku.*	１万人の仲間の固い結束。	*EE-chee MA-nin-no nah-KA-mah no ka-TAI KESS-koo*

We find joy and harmony around the clock!	*Tokei no ugoki ni yorokobi to chowa ga kizamareru!*	時計の動き に喜びと 調和が 刻まれる！	*Toh-KAY no WOO-go-kee nee yo-roh-KOH-bee toh CHO-wa ga KEE-za-ma-RAY-roo!*
We never contradict our superiors!	*Uwayaku to shototsu shinai!*	上役と衝突 しない！	*OO-wa-YA-koo toh SHOTE-tsoo shee-NAI!*
Happiness for all people as company grows ever larger.	*Kaisha no hatten wa jibun no seicho da.*	会社の 発展は自分の 成長だ。	*KAI-sha no HA-ten wa jee-BUN no SAY-cho da.*
And finally swallows entire planet!	*Chikyu o nomikomo!*	地球をのみ こもう！	*Cheek-yoo oh no-MEE-ko-MO!*

STALKING THE DEAL ¥

BOW TO CONQUER

The Japanese expect handshakes from *gaijin*. To them we are barbarians who could never grasp the excruciating subtleties of the bow. Attempts at bowing are appreciated, however, and can do much to ingratiate you with the natives.

A proper bow is crisp and made from the waist—it is not a nod. Hold your arms stiffly at your sides, as if you were offering to have your head chopped off. In close quarters, bow at an angle to avoid knocking your opponent unconscious.

Pause slightly at the bottom of your bow, both to show respect and to examine the quality of your counterpart's footwear. Rank is not always obvious, but you should assume that people wearing shoes more expensive and well-polished than your own outrank you. Bow longer and more deeply to them.

But whatever you do, don't take bowing too seriously. The Japanese study it their whole lives; you cannot ever hope to become totally proficient. Mastering the mechanical details is difficult and adopting the proper attitude is close to impossible.

FLIGHT OF THE CRANE AND THE PROPER INTRODUCTION

In Japan, a man is his work. A *meishi* (business card) therefore sums up a person's identity and value as a human being; treat it with respect.

Your own card should be printed in English on one side and Japanese on the other. (Your hotel can print proper cards in 24 hours.) Upon introduction, pull a card from its special case in a single smooth motion without excessive flourish, much as the crane takes wing on a winter morning. Bow as you exchange cards, holding yours in such a way so that the recipient can read it.

After completing your bow, study the card of your new associate carefully. Make a little light conversation.

Happy to make your acquaintance.	*Oai dekite saiwai desu.*	お会いでき て幸いです。	*Oh-AI day-KEE-tay SAI-wai DAY-soo.*

STALKING THE DEAL ¥

I see you work for the largest bank on the planet.	*Sekai ichi no ginko ni otsutome desune.*	世界一の銀行にお勤めですね。	*Seh-KAI EE-chee no gheen-KO nee OAT-soo-TOH-may dess-NAY.*
Yes, I hope to do business here in Japan.	*Hai, nihon de shigoto o shitai to nozonde imasu.*	ハイ、日本で仕事をしたいと望んでいます。	*Hai, NEE-hone day shee-GO-toh oh shee-TAI toh NO-zohn-day ee-MOSS.*
Thank you, yes, I could use a little help.	*Arigato gozaimasu. Gokyoryoku itadakereba saiwai desu.*	ありがとうございます。御協力いただければ幸いです。	*AH-ree-GA-toh GO-zai-MOSS. Goke-YO-ree-OH-koo ee-TA-da-KAY-ray-ba SAI-wai dess.*
I wish to have the advantages of Japanese business people.	*Nihon no bizinesu no katagata no ochikara ga hitsuyo desu.*	日本のビジネスの方々のお力が必要です。	*NEE-hone no BEE-zoo-NESS-oo no KAH-tah-GA-tah no OH-chee-KA-ra ga heet-SOO-yo DAY-soo.*
Could you lend me 10 billion yen at 4% interest?	*Hyakuoku-yen, risoku yon-pasento de kashite moraemasuka?*	100億円、利息4％で貸してもらえますか？	*Hai-YA-koo-OH-koo-yen, ree-SO-koo you-PA-sent-oh day ka-SHEE-tay MO-ray-MOSS-ka?*

TRANSLATING ATTITUDES

Japanese business decisions are based on trust and long-term relationships, not on price or quality. To win that trust, you have to play the game their way.

Many of the qualities we value in our salespeople are disastrous in Japan, so you must learn how attitudes translate between cultures.

WESTERN ATTITUDE	JAPANESE TRANSLATION
Confident	Boastful
Direct	Crude
Open	Foolish
Forceful	Pushy
Eager	Weak
Anxious	Defeated

JAPANESE ATTITUDE	WESTERN TRANSLATION
Powerful	Inert
Strong	Intransigent
Patient	Catatonic
Harmonious	Soul-less
Superior	Ridiculous
Fun	Drunken
Clever	Two-faced

THE FIRST BUSINESS MEETING

When doing business, always wear a conservative dark suit with white shirt and blue tie. The Japanese are frightened by individualism. To them, a light blue shirt is rebellious and shocking.

One should never discuss business in the first business meeting. That would be considered rude and forward, even if you spent a year setting it up.

Pleased to meet you at last!	*Yoyaku oai deki mashitane!*	ようやく お会いでき ましたね！	*YO-ee-AH-koo oh-AI DEK-ee mosh-TA-nay!*
So sorry to disturb your busy schedule!	*Ojama shite sumimasen!*	お邪魔して すみません！	*Oh-JAH-ma SHEE-tay soo-mee-MA-sen!*
These are handsome offices.	*Suteki na ofisu desune.*	すてきな オフィス ですね。	*Soo-TEK-ee na oh-FEE-soo dess-NAY.*
Say! How about those Tokyo Giants*/ Osaka Tigers!	*Iya, jaiantsu/ taigasu no katsuyakuburi wa dodesu!*	いやー、ジ ャイアンツ /タイガ ースの 活躍ぶりは どうです！	*EE-ya jai-AHN-tsu/tai-GA-soo no KAHT-so-YAH-koo-boo-ree wa doh-DESS!*
Quite a ball team!	*Sugoi chimu desu yone!*	すごい チームです よね！	*Soo-GOY CHEE-moo DAY-soo YO-nay!*

💴 STALKING THE DEAL

Well, we must be going.	*Ah, mo shitsurei seneba narimasen.*	あー、もう失礼せねばなりません。	*Ah, mo sheet-SOO-ray sen-AY-ba NAH-ree-MA-sen.*
We must catch a plane for our 20-hour, $3,000 flight home.	*Ofuku yonjumanen haratta hikoki de, nijujikan kakete kaerimasu.*	往復40万円払った飛行機で、20時間かけて帰ります。	*OAF-oo-koo yone-JOO-ma-nen ha-RA-tah hee-KOH-kee day, nee-JOO-jee-kahn ka-KAY-tay KAY-ree-MOSS.*
An honor to meet you!	*Ome ni kakarete koei deshita!*	お眼にかかれて光栄でした！	*OH-may nee ka-ka-RAY-tay KOH-ay DESH-tah!*
We'll look you up again when we happen to find ourselves across the Pacific Ocean!	*Moshi kochira ni kuru kikai ga areba mata yorasete itadaki masu!*	もしこちらに来る機会があればまた寄らせていただきます！	*MOSH-ee ko-chee-ra nee KOO-roo kee-KAI ga ah-RAY-ba MA-tah YO-ra-SAY-tay ee-tah-DA-kee MOSS!*

*Never mention the Giants outside of Tokyo.

STALKING THE DEAL 💴

SUMO-STYLE SALES TECHNIQUES

Sumo wrestling has direct parallels to business in
Japan. Opponents test each other's character for
what seems like ages, trying to gain psychological
advantage, focusing on small details and avoiding
direct confrontation. To the Japanese, a negotiation is like a *torikumi*: there's a winner and a
loser.

The pushing and shoving of the final hours of
negotiation are made of threats and ultimatums.
Give as good as you get, and remember that the
Japanese don't take ultimatums seriously.

I'm afraid we cannot accept your proposal.	*Anata no goyobo niwa okotae dekikane masu.*	あなたの 御要望には お応えでき かねます。	*Ah-NAH-ta no go-yo-bo NEE-wa oh-KOH-tay DEK-ee-KAY-nay MOSS-en.*
We cannot return home with such a deal.	*Sonna joken dewa kuni ewa kaeremasen.*	そんな条件 では、国へは 帰れません。	*SO-nah jo-ken DAY-wa koo-nee AY-wa ka-AY-ray-MOSS-en.*
To lift the shame from our firm and families, we would all be forced to kill ourselves.	*Shinde kaisha to kazoku ni owabi shimasu.*	死んで会社 と家族に おわび します。	*SHIN-day KAI-shah toh ka-ZOKE nee oh-WA-bee shee-MOSS.*

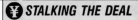

We offered you the moon.	*Tsuki o kaimasenka.*	月を買い ませんか。	*TSOO-kee oh KAI-ma-SENK-ah.*
But you want Jupiter, Mars and Dolly Parton, too.	*Mokusei to kasei to dori paton mo onozomi desuka.*	木星と火星 とドリー・ パートンも お望みで すか。	*MOKE-say toh ka-SAY toh doh-REE PAT-on mo own-ZOH-me DESK-ah.*
Goodbye, gentlemen.	*Sayonara, minasan.*	さようなら、 みなさん。	*SIGH-oh-NAH-rah, MEE-nah-sahn.*
What? We misunder-stood?	*EH? Gokai ga aru?*	えっ？誤解 がある？	*Eh? Go-KAI ga AH-roo?*
Fire the translator! Let's sit back down!	*Tsuyaku o kubi ni shiro! Mo ichido hanashiai masho!*	通訳をクビ にしろ！ もう一度話し 合いまし ょう！	*TSOO-ya-koo oh koo-bee nee SHEE-roh! Mo ee-CHEE-doh ha-NAH-shee-AI ma-SHO!*

INTERPRETING NON-VERBAL SIGNALS

Just as the Japanese language is different from our own, so are the hand gestures and facial expressions.

SIGNAL	MEANING
A sharp, exhaling breath and a breaking of eye contact.	*"I find it hard to accept or understand what you are saying."*
Smiling.	*"You make me uncomfortable."*
Long, stone-faced silence.	*"We are considering your proposal."*
Even longer silence.	*"Don't rush us."*
Snoring.	*"Your deadline approaches, yes?"*
Shaking finger at someone.	*"I have hostile feelings."*
Pointing finger at own chest.	*"I want to fight you."*
Coming across table, shouting, "Tawake!"	*"Your proposal is not pleasing."*

NEVER JUST SAY NO

Japanese negotiators will test you by asking for unilateral concessions. DO NOT GIVE IN. The smallest unilateral concession will convince your opponents that you are the moral equivalent of a sea cucumber, fit not for battle but for soup.

Still, since harmony must be preserved at all costs, you must never say no.

Good idea.	*Ee kangae desu.*	いい考え です。	*ee KON-gay gay DAY-soo.*
You are very generous.	*Goshinsetsu arigato.*	御親切あり がとう。	*GO-shin-SET-soo AH-ree-GA-toh.*
I will be happy to reveal trade secrets for free.	*Tada de shobai no himitsu o ooshie shimasho.*	タダで商売 の秘密を お教えしま しょう。	*TA-da day sho-BAI no hee-MEET-soo oh OH-shee SHEE-ma-SHOW.*
It would certainly excite my colleagues back home.	*Kore o kuni no doryo ga kiitara bikkuri shimasu.*	これを国の 同僚がきい たらビッ クリします。	*KOH-ray oh KOO-nee no DOOR-ee-oh ga kee-TA-rah BEE-koo-ree shee-MOSS.*

STALKING THE DEAL 💴

Change the meeting time by 10 minutes?	*Miitingu no jikan o juppun henkou suruno desuka?*	ミーティングの時間を10分変更するのですか？	*MEE-teen-goo no jee-KAHN oh joo-POON hen-KOH soo- ROO-no DESK-ah.*
My colleagues are certain to like that idea.	*Dooryo mo yoi an dato iukoto desho.*	同僚も良い案だという事でしょう。	*DOH-ree-yoh mo yoy ahn DA-toh YOO-koh-toh DESH-oh.*
I will consult with them.	*Minato soudan itashimasu.*	皆と相談いたします。	*Mee-NA-toh SO-dahn EE-ta-shee-MA-soo.*
Then I will arrange a conference call to get permission from my superiors at the home office.	*Honsha no uwayaku karano kyokka o erutameno denwa o kakemasho.*	本社の上役からの許可を得るための電話をかけましょう。	*HONE-shah no OO-wa-YA-koo ka-RA-no KYO-ka oh ay-roo-TA-may-no DEN-wa oh ka-kay-ma-SHOW.*
When shall we meet to discuss your time-change proposal?	*Jikan no henkou ni tsuite itsu oaishite hanasemasuka?*	時間の変更について何時お会いして話せますか？	*Jee-KAHN no hen-KO nee TSOO-ee-tay EET-soo oh-AYSH-tay HA-nah-say-MOSS-kah?*